D0947106

347CSG /SS
BASE LIBRARY/FL4830
MOODY AFB, GA. 31699

LITTLE TURTLE

By Maggi Cunningham

DILLON PRESS, INC.
MINNEAPOLIS, MINNESOTA

©1978 by Dillon Press, Inc. All rights reserved
Second printing 1980

Dillon Press, Inc., 500 South Third Street
Minneapolis, Minnesota 55415

Printed in the United States of America

Library of Congress Cataloging in Publication Data

Cunningham, Maggi, 1916-
  Little Turtle.

  (The Story of an American Indian)
  SUMMARY: A biography of the Miami Indian chief who
formed a confederation of Miami, Shawnee, and Potawatomi
Indians that unsuccessfully attempted to drive white settlers
from tribal lands.
  1. Little Turtle, Miami chief, d. 1812—Juvenile literature.
2. Miami Indians—Biography—Juvenile literature. 3. Indians
of North America—Wars—1790-1794—Juvenile literature.
[1. Little Turtle, Miami chief, d. 1812. 2. Miami Indians—
Biography. 3. Indians of North America—Biography] I. Title.
E99.M48L485   970'.004'97 [B]   77-16764
ISBN 0-87518-158-9

U.S. AIR FORCE

ON THE COVER:
A portrait of Little Turtle by K. Matchey

LITTLE TURTLE

Little Turtle, a hereditary chief of the Miamis living in what became the states of Indiana, Ohio, and Michigan, formed an Indian confederation to repel white settlers who were invading the Maumee Basin, lands guaranteed by the Proclamation of 1787 to belong to the Indians forever. A brilliant leader and skilled military strategist, Little Turtle fought several campaigns until the confederation was finally defeated by General Anthony Wayne at the Battle of Fallen Timbers in 1794.

As he confronted Wayne across the treaty table, he vowed, "I am the last to sign this treaty. I promise I will be the last to break it." Thereafter he taught the Miamis to combine the best of the white people's ways with their own. His people were not dealt with so honorably. In 1846 they were driven from their homeland to follow "The Trail of Tears" to the Indian territory in the Southwest.

Contents

CHAPTER I

The
People

On a bright day in the early autumn of 1812, a guard of honor from the army of the United States rode into the village that had grown up around the home of Little Turtle, the great Miami war chief. They were soldiers from the garrison at Fort Wayne, and they had traveled twenty miles to this place on the Maumee River in Ohio.

The captain had stopped his men back among the trees so they could shake all the dust from their uniforms. Their hands and faces were washed, and their boots were polished. The coats of the horses had been groomed until they shone like satin. Reins and harness had been rubbed with oil. Rifles, spotlessly clean, rested in holsters that hung from saddles of leather that had been buffed to a sheen. Everything sparkled in the sunshine.

The captain and his men rode slowly across the field where the corn had already been cut. They were careful not to let their horses step on the pumpkins that were ripening on the ground. Only a few years before, they would have come up to the village as enemies. There would have been a defense, and blood would have been shed on both sides. Now, thanks to the peacekeeping efforts of Little Turtle, the man they had come to honor, the captain knew they would be welcomed as visitors by all who lived there.

A scout had brought word that the army was coming, and the oldest man in the village was at the open gate of the palisade to meet them. The old man escorted the captain through the village and ushered him into the council hut where all the chiefs were waiting.

Everybody sat quietly for a while, giving the newcomer time to feel at ease. A pipe was passed and, after it had gone around, the oldest man stood up and made a short speech welcoming the United States army to the village of Little Turtle.

When the village elder sat down, it was the captain's turn. He told the chiefs that President James Madison was saddened when he learned that the soul of Little Turtle had been gathered up by the Great Spirit. He had sent a rider to the garrison at Fort Wayne with the command that a full ceremony of military honor was to be carried out at the grave of the great war chief.

The chiefs nodded at each other, and one spoke for all. He pointed to the wampum belts that were hanging on the inside walls of the council hut.

Wampum was a bead carved from wood or shell, and strings or belts of wampum were given and received between Indians as sacred symbols of promises made, agreements to be lived up to, and honors to be paid. Before the white people came, the Indians had no need for money. Wampum was a pledge of honor. White wampum meant peace and good will. Wampum that was black or marked with red was the symbol of disagreement or war.

Most of the belts on the walls were "fathom" belts, as long as the spread of a man's arms. Ever since the death of

Little Turtle on July 14, 1812, these tributes had been coming in from tribes as far away as New York.

The chief said the Miamis were proud to hear the good words of the president, but the burial ground of the nation was sacred. It must not be marked by the footprint of a stranger. According to the Miami way, the body of Little Turtle had been put in a secret place in the burial ground. The Americans were welcome, however, to show respect in their own way. As long as they did not break the custom!

All the people in the village came to watch as the captain called his men to attention outside the palisade on the bank of the river. There was a flurry of muffled drums, and a bugler sounded a few clear notes. The captain unrolled a piece of parchment and read the words of President Madison praising Little Turtle as a gallant enemy in war and a firm friend in peace. When he had finished, the soldiers aimed their rifles toward the sky and, at a command, fired a volley. They did that three times, making a racket that sent frightened birds screaming through the trees. The captain drew his sword, placed the hilt to his lips in a formal salute, and returned it to its scabbard. He bowed and handed a folded American flag to the oldest man. Then he gave a command for his men to mount up, and they rode away into the forest.

The flag was taken to the council hut, unfolded, and hung on the wall beside the wampum belts. It was right that the Americans should honor Little Turtle. Ever since the Treaty of Greenville was signed, he had urged the Miamis to accept the fact that the white settlers should be allowed to live in peace on hunting grounds they had thought of as their own.

The Indians had been brave in trying to defend their lands, but bravery was no match for the great numbers of whites who were crossing the ocean to come to America and join those already there. If the Miamis were to survive as a people, they must learn to live with their new neighbors.

The Miamis had lived in their part of what the Americans called the Northwest Territory since the time the Great Spirit had shaped the earth with his hands. He had given them hunting grounds that began in Indiana and crossed Ohio into Michigan. They covered the upper basin of the Maumee River and part of the valley of the Wabash River.

North of the Miami country, Ottawas and Wyandots lived along Lake Erie. To the southeast, there were the Shawnees. Mingos, an offshoot of the Iroquois, the long-house people, lived between the Shawnees and the Delawares. The Potawatomis were off to the west. Trails, strewn with white sand and deeply worn, criss-crossed the land between Lake Erie and the Ohio River.

The Miamis and their neighbors belonged to the Algonquin language family. "Algonquin" came from an Indian word, *Alligewinenk,* meaning "come from distant parts." The language family reached from the eastern mountains to the Mississippi River. It was divided into clans in which all members were related by blood. Each clan had its own chief. The clans, banded together, formed a tribe. All the tribes made up a nation. When the Indians spoke of themselves, they called themselves The People.

The Miamis, who were farmers and hunters, lived in organized villages. The houses were the same oblong shape as the longhouses of their eastern language cousins, only smaller. Usually, only one family lived in a house.

A Miami lodge was supported by a framework of sturdy saplings (top) and covered by reed mats (bottom).

Like the longhouses, the sides and curved roofs were covered with mats woven from the dried stalks of cattails that grew along the river bottoms or with shingles cut from the bark of elm trees.

The houses were arranged around a stomp ground where ceremonial dances were performed and where a fire always burned. The whole village was surrounded by a wall of logs driven into the ground and sharpened at the top. They were set so close together that no enemy could squeeze through.

Outside the wall were fields of corn, beans, squash, and pumpkins. Corn was the greatest food gift the Miamis had received from the Great Spirit, the Master of Life. He had placed its care entirely in the hands of the women, and they made sure that no part of the gift was wasted.

When the corn was still green, the kernels could be stripped from the ears and roasted or boiled. Ripe, they were dried and stored or pounded into meal. Sometimes, they were "popped" for a treat for the children to eat while they played with dolls made of corn cobs, dressed in corn leaves with corn silk for hair.

While the corn was growing, the strong, slender stalks supported the vines of the beans that had been planted in the same bed. After the harvest, the dry stalks and empty cobs were burned for fuel.

Beyond the fields were forests where the men of the tribe hunted animals for meat and furs to feed and clothe their families. There were great herds of deer as well as bears, panthers, wild cats, foxes, raccoons, muskrats, beavers, squirrels, and opossums. There were wolves, too, but a wolf was sacred and never killed.

The women guarded the cornfields to keep crows and animals from destroying their crops.

The air above the forest carried flocks of wild ducks, geese, swans, pigeons, and turkeys. The rivers and creeks were full of fish. Droves of wild ponies roamed the prairies beyond the forests.

There were wild strawberries, blackberries, raspberries, grapes, plums, blueberries, and black currants to be picked. Hazel and hickory nuts, chestnuts, black walnuts, and acorns to be gathered. There was even a tree whose sap could be boiled down to make sugar!

The Great Spirit had given the Miami Indians a true land of plenty to be their home.

The Miamis were a religious people. They knew that the Great Spirit showed himself in the sun and in thunderstorms when his fire could strike down a tree. Every important activity began with rites designed to catch his attention and ask for his help.

Even war was a ritual with rules and courtesies that must be followed. The Miamis never made war unless their hunting grounds were threatened. Then, before a war party went out to meet an enemy, they gathered for prayers and ceremonial dances at the stomp ground.

Once in the field, a warrior gained honor if he could count coup. That meant that he had put his hand on the enemy and lived to tell about it. It was much more dangerous to touch than to kill. The violent games the Indians played for fun were likely to be more bloody and end up with more broken bones than war.

A captive taken in war or on a raid was treated with respect by the warriors. Once they brought him back to their village, however, he was forced to face the challenge of the gauntlet.

Women, children, and old men, armed with sticks and clubs, formed two lines, and the captive had to run as fast as he could between them to reach the safety of a house at the end. If he succeeded—and most did—he would probably be adopted into a clan that had lost a warrior.

Or he might be ransomed by an unattached woman. The women of the Algonquin language family had great influence. The family house and everything in it belonged to the oldest married woman, and all men traced their ancestry through their mothers.

Female captives were never sent down the gauntlet. Instead, they found homes with the tribes which had taken them. They might join a family to help around the house or, if a warrior had lost his wife through sickness or an accident, the captive might marry him. If she liked him.

Sometimes, an important captive was given the honor of being sacrificed to the sun, in which the Great Spirit showed himself. The Indians believed that a person's soul lived on after the body and the courage with which a warrior met his fate gave him honor in the Land Above the Sky. But Little Turtle thought that human life was a great gift, and he argued that the Great Spirit did not want human sacrifices. Before his death in 1812, the practice was almost stopped.

The Miamis were a good-looking people. They were of average height or taller with rosy, copper-colored skin. In warm weather, the men wore no clothing except deerskin leggings and breechclouts. That was so they could show off their tattoo marks. Every adventure or brave deed in a man's life was marked on his skin in a design or a picture-story. By the time a man was middle-aged, his entire body might be covered with patterns. In the winter time, he wore a fur robe or a woolen blanket which he had bartered from a trader.

The women, on the other hand, were always well clothed. Their knee-length sheathes were made of deerskin that had been treated until it was soft as velvet and decorated with painted designs or patterns embroidered with porcupine quills and edged with fringe.

The Miami Indians were not warlike, but they were skillful raiders. In groups of ten to twenty, they would swoop down on the village of another tribe and carry off whatever took their fancy. Among themselves, however, they were polite and pleasant and respectful and obedient to their chiefs. They loved to wrestle, but their favorite sport was running. News of a footrace in a Miami village brought crowds from everywhere. The Miamis liked to gamble, and the betting would be heavy on the favorites among the contestants.

These were the people among whom the noble war chief, Little Turtle, was born, grew up, and became a great leader. Because of his fame, the Miami Indians of the Maumee River Basin will be remembered forever.

CHAPTER II

The New Chief

Little Turtle, whose proper Indian name was Michikinikwa, was born in 1752, in the Miami village of Piquawillani. The village was built near the place where Laramie Creek empties into the Great Miami River. Today, it is the site of the town of Piqua, Ohio. His father was the respected chief, Kequnacquan. His mother was a Mohican woman whom Kequnacquan had captured on a raid.

Memory holds nothing of Little Turtle's boyhood years, so his childhood name is not known. He would have been given his childhood name when his parents carried a string of wampum and a food sacrifice to the oldest person in the village. While the sacrifice was being accepted and blessed, a friend of the parents sang a song telling the name chosen for the new baby.

By the time a boy was old enough to go out with the raiders, he had selected his manhood name. A man chose his name based on a dream or some event that had made him feel the presence of the Great Spirit.

Then, as with his childhood name, wampum and a food sacrifice were carried to be blessed by the oldest person in the village, and a friend sang a song that told everybody the name by which the man was to be known.

Young Little Turtle may have practiced his marksmanship by shooting at fish.

That name was never spoken in his presence. It was a part of his spirit and was used to represent him when he was absent.

Little Turtle's choice was thought to be a lucky name. An ancient legend of the Algonquin language family told about The People being caught in a flood that covered the whole earth. They climbed onto the back of a great turtle and lived there until the water went down. Then, because it can move on land as well as in the water, the turtle carried The People to dry land. After that, the turtle was given much respect, and the fact that Little Turtle had met one in his dream was thought to be a good sign.

When Little Turtle was ready to go out with the war parties and join the raiders, the seasoned warriors were pleased with his courage and daring. When the time came for him to lead his own parties, he planned every detail of the action with care. He tried to put himself inside the minds of the enemies so he could guess how they would act. Older men began to ask his advice before they went out on their own raids.

As a young warrior, Little Turtle was able to count coup many times. It was the dream of many a young Shawnee or a Delaware to be able to count coup against the Miami, Little Turtle, but he was nimble and able to move very fast. Only a few succeeded.

All the time Little Turtle was growing up, a constant stream of French and English traders came through his village. They brought cooking pots, cloth, tomahawks, and knives as well as guns and bullets. They took away grain, vegetables, and fortunes in furs which the Indians used for barter.

Little Turtle worked with every new thing the traders brought. He became an expert marksman with guns as well as with bows and arrows. He began to make his own knives and tomahawks, using the ones the traders brought as models, and improving on them. Little Turtle and the men who went with him on raids had the best weapons of all the Miamis.

The young warrior was most interested when the traders talked about the new nation, the United States of America, that was growing strong to the east of the rivers The People knew. He was surprised at the difference between the way Indian war parties fought and the methods used by the Americans.

White men could be trained to march, each man even with the one next to him, all using their right and left feet at the same time. They waited to fire their rifles until the leader gave a command, and then they all fired at once. It was very puzzling to a young Indian who was used to fighting by himself and not as part of a group.

Little Turtle wanted to learn everything he could about the white people who were moving closer every day to the hunting grounds of The People. His father, Kequnacquan, had traveled as far as Philadelphia, the principal city of the new nation, and he had brought back some strange tales.

When Little Turtle became a grown man, he was almost six feet tall, slender, and muscular. He had a thin face with a high forehead, level brows above full, dark eyes that sparkled with intelligence and good humor, a narrow nose with a slightly high bridge, and a wide curving mouth. In any group of men, Little Turtle would stand out as a leader.

That was the reason why the people in the village of

Piquawillani took so much interest in a council that was going on in the hut, one fine spring day. The women were not in the fields as usual. The men had not gone hunting in the forest, and even the children were playing close to home. Everybody stood around and watched the smoke rising from the vent in the roof of the council hut. That meant the meeting was still going on.

Inside the hut, the chiefs of the clans and the old men were sitting around a small fire. They had talked of many things, but the most important had been left to the last. A pipe was passed around the circle and, after a few minutes of polite silence, the oldest man present asked the question, "Shall Little Turtle, whose proper Indian name is Michikinikwa, and whose father, the Chief Kequnacquan, has been taken away by the sickness of old men, be named hereditary chief of the Miamis in his place?"

Ordinarily, there would have been no such question, especially in the case of a young man as beloved and respected as Little Turtle. The reason it was asked was because his mother had been a Mohican. Since a man's blood line was traced through his mother, Little Turtle was, by blood, a Mohican.

It was true that Little Turtle's wife was a Miami and their two children would inherit a place in the tribe, his daughter through her own right and his son through his mother. But what about Little Turtle himself? Should the council go against tradition and name him a chief?

Then, one of the men reminded the others that they didn't have to make the decision all by themselves. Any chief—even an hereditary one—had to have the approval of the women of the tribe.

No woman sat in the council circle, but the headwoman of the village was always invited to give advice and report the opinions of all the other women whenever an important decision had to be made.

The women of the village of Piquawillani had had their meeting earlier, and the headwoman was ready when she was called to the council hut. She entered and listened while the men told her about their problem. Then they asked her if the women of the clans felt that Little Turtle should take the place of his father, Kequnacquan, as an hereditary chief of the Miami Indians even though—by blood—he was a Mohican.

The headwoman's answer was a firm *yes*. She went on to say that, when sons, husbands, and brothers went on a raid with Little Turtle, he brought most of them back alive.

Little Turtle had introduced something new into Indian raids—silence. Instead of whooping and yelling so that everyone knew they were coming, Little Turtle gave orders that his men must remain quiet until they were right on top of their target. That way, they were able to do what they had come to do and get away before the surprise had worn off. He did bring most of the men back to their families.

She asked if the tribe wanted to take a chance on losing such a leader. Surely, if Little Turtle was not accepted as a chief, he would leave the village and not a few of the young men would go with him.

It did not take many more words for the people in the council hut to know that they were all in agreement. They called Little Turtle in to tell him that he was a new chief of the Miami Indians.

He entered the hut and stood before the council. For a minute, nobody spoke. Then, the oldest man got to his feet, handed the young man a belt of wampum, and spoke his new title, "Little Turtle, Chief of the Miamis!"

All the others heaped wampum on the new chief, and they made so much happy noise that the people listening outside guessed what had happened. The council had made the decision that everybody wanted.

When Little Turtle came out of the council hut, the first person to hand him a string of precious white wampum and offer good wishes was William Wells, his adopted son.

Little Turtle and his band of raiders had been on a raid in Kentucky when they met eleven-year-old William Wells playing by himself in the forest. All children, regardless of the color of their skin, were a delight to the Miamis. Little Turtle scooped him up and took him home to be a playmate for his own children.

William came from a good family in Kentucky, and Little Turtle could have asked for a ransom. The Indians had learned that the white people didn't understand the challenge of the gauntlet and had no reverence for the sun. Since those honors were wasted on them, white captives were allowed to be ransomed by their own people.

But William didn't want to go home! He liked living with the Miamis and quickly became Little Turtle's shadow, walking in his moccasin prints and copying his idol in every way he could.

Little Turtle was fond of young William Wells. He adopted him as a son and took him into his family. The boy often acted as his interpreter when travelers or traders came to the village. After a while, William taught Little

William Wells, the adopted son of Little Turtle, who would one day have to choose between his Indian and white families.

Turtle to speak English so the Miami Indian could talk to the white neighbors himself, not through the mouth of another man.

As soon as the boy was old enough, he went along on Little Turtle's raids and rode with the Miami war parties. William Wells and Little Turtle were always together. They lived in the same house, hunted together, and rode side by side. William taught Little Turtle as much as he could remember about the ways of the white people—how they lived, what they believed, and why they acted the way they did. The Miami warrior and the young white man were faithful friends and constant companions.

CHAPTER III

The Clenched Fist

In 1787, when Little Turtle was twenty-five years old, the Congress of the United States issued a proclamation. It declared that land in the Northwest Territory that was east of the Mississippi River and north of the Ohio was to belong to the Indians forever. That included the Maumee River Basin which covered parts of Indiana, Ohio, and Michigan.

Since the time before memory, that area had been the hunting ground of the Miami Indians. Their homes, fields, and burial grounds were there. They were puzzled by these new white people who pretended to give them what they had already received from the Great Spirit. Still, all land belonged to the Great Spirit so there must be enough for everybody. If that proclamation made the United States government happy, what difference could it make?

It was to make a tragic difference. The land in the Maumee Basin was rich with natural drainage from water that ran from many creeks and rivers into lakes. Travelers from the east went home with stories about prairies covered with fields of corn and beans that grew in the sun and rain without anybody doing any work. They talked about rivers with names like Scioto, Olentangy, Auglaize, and Muskingum that were so deep and wide that boats could ride on them. They told of creeks nearly as big as the rivers and so full of fish that they could be caught by dipping a hand in the water. There were vast forests where fortunes in deerskins and the pelts of bear, fox, muskrat, and beaver hid in every shadow.

News of such easy wealth tempted the greedy, the adventurous, and the ambitious. Soon all kinds of people were quietly moving onto the Indian lands. In less than three years after Congress had set the boundaries, more than twenty thousand white settlers had entered illegally and were building homes on land that had been set aside to belong to the Indians forever. Forts and towns grew up along the rivers, and the tribes saw their hunting grounds cut in two.

The situation was one in which the British saw a chance to make trouble for the United States. Although the Revolutionary War was over and the Treaty of Paris had been signed, the British kept a string of forts along the Great Lakes. The forts were disguised as trading posts, but they really were hiding places for stores of guns and bullets.

English traders went among the Indians in the Maumee Basin, carrying stories about the Americans who were coming to settle on Indian lands. They advised the tribes to fight the white invaders, and they promised to supply all the guns and bullets the Indians would need. In secret, of course!

At first, the Indians had been surprised at the boldness of the whites who came to live on their hunting grounds. When the settlers began driving clans from their villages and plowing up the burial grounds to plant fields, a deep

Five states and part of a sixth would be carved out of the Northwest Territory, created by an act of Congress in 1787. Places and events of importance in Little Turtle's story are shown on the map. (Not to scale.)

The settlers turned the game-filled forests into fields. Here they are burning down trees which they have killed by "girdling," or chopping a ring out of the living wood of the trunks.

anger came on The People. They were happy to accept the help which the English offered.

Both settlers and Indians did cruel things to each other. The Indians burned the homesteads of the settlers, killed them, or took them captive to be held for ransom. At the same time, at Gnadenhutten, in Delaware country, white men from Pennsylvania massacred a group of peaceful Indians who had been converted to Christianity. Among the slain was the Delaware chief, Netawatwees, who had been baptised with the Christian name of Abraham. The only reason the Pennsylvanians gave for the killing was that the people were Indians!

Little Turtle, with William Wells at his side, led war parties in raids against the settlements. He watched chiefs of the Shawnees, the Delawares, and the other tribes fighting the same small battles. They all did the best they could, but it never seemed to be enough. No sooner was one group of settlers driven out than another took its place. Scattered bands of Indians could not deal with the great numbers of white invaders.

Little Turtle began to feel sure that the Miamis and the other tribes were going about protecting their homes and hunting grounds in the wrong way. He worked out a plan that might succeed if he could get the others to go along with it.

He sent invitations for a council to all the principal tribes that lived in the Maumee Basin. Little Turtle was known to be a fine orator and chiefs of the Delawares, Shawnees, and Potawatomis came for the pleasure of listening to him speak.

He began by reminding them that the land on which they lived had been given to their ancestors by the Great Spirit. Then Little Turtle challenged them to count up the losses in people, land, and belongings that each tribe had suffered as it tried to drive off the invaders by itself. Now, he asked them, why did each tribe fight its own lonely war? Because petty squabbles, differences, and long-standing feuds were keeping them apart!

Little Turtle told the chiefs that the time had come for them to make peace with one another. Each man looked at the one sitting beside him. Did the chief of the Miamis mean that they were to forget the quarrels that had been handed down from father to son?

That was exactly what Little Turtle meant. Instead of fighting with one another, they must unite and make war only on the one enemy that threatened all of them.

It was Little Turtle's idea that the Indians in the Maumee River Basin should unite into a confederation and show a solid front to the white settlers. Instead of small war parties, a confederation could call up a hundred—even a thousand —warriors.

To show the chiefs what he meant, Little Turtle put out his hand with the fingers spread. He showed them how easily each finger could be broken. It was the same with the tribes. Then he clenched his fist and raised it above his head. Gathered together like his fingers, the tribes would be a powerful weapon!

The chiefs who had come to the council saw that Little Turtle's idea had much wisdom, and they were in favor of putting it into action at once. The Miami chief reminded them that if they were going to succeed, even the smallest tribe must be included. He offered to travel to all the villages in the Maumee Basin and explain the confederation.

Blue Jacket, a powerful chief of the Shawnees and a man with a short and violent temper, declared he would go along. So did Buckongehalos, a sachem of the Delawares whose name meant "breaker into small pieces." Although Buckongehalos was ready to fight, he longed for peace. He would be a good balance for the fierce Blue Jacket.

The Indian confederacy became a reality. Little Turtle was everybody's choice to be war chief, and he was given the council bag which was the symbol of his authority. Blue Jacket and Buckongehalos were selected as his seconds-in-command.

Little Turtle began planning his campaign against the whites with attention to the smallest detail. He sent men out to round up the wild ponies that roamed the prairies and set about taming them so there would be replacements for his mounted warriors to ride. Food, guns, and bullets were stockpiled in safe places.

There were no more hit-and-run attacks by small bands of Indians. Each encounter with the whites was to be a battle with every move plotted well ahead and fought at the place and time selected by Little Turtle.

The confederation became so successful that some home-steaders packed up their belongings and headed back east without ever seeing an Indian. Would-be settlers began to have second thoughts about entering the Maumee Basin.

In Philadelphia, President George Washington was caught between the pledge the U.S. government had made to the Indians and the Americans who were demanding protection when they settled on the rich lands they were stealing from the Indians.

All his life, Washington tried to shield the Indians and deal with them in a fair manner. Congress had appointed General Arthur St. Clair, a model soldier in the Revolution, to be governor of the Northwest Territory. The president sent word to St. Clair that he was to talk with the Indians and offer to buy some of their land so the Americans could move in.

St. Clair made his headquarters in the settlement of Marietta on the Ohio River. He sent invitations to the chiefs of all the tribes in the Maumee Basin to come to a council to be held at the place where the Muskingum River flowed into the Ohio.

The message that went to Little Turtle was most friendly. St. Clair knew all about the confederation and that Little

The house in Marietta, Ohio, where General St. Clair lived. At one time during the Indian war, it sheltered two hundred frightened settlers.

Turtle was the man who had put it together. If Little Turtle didn't accept the invitation, St. Clair would have to face the fact that his council was not going to be a success.

On the chosen day, the governor watched eagerly as chiefs from some of the invited tribes straggled in. He waited until the sun went down, but there was no sign of the Miami war chief. Blue Jacket, the Shawnee, did not come, either. Nor did Buckongehalos, the Delaware.

The next morning, Governor St. Clair knew that it was hopeless to wait any longer. He might as well make the best of a disappointing situation. He went out to give President Washington's message to the chiefs who were waiting. All he could do was hope for the best.

Wearing his army uniform and all his medals, Arthur St.

Clair stood before the Indians and told them that the Great Father in Philadelphia wanted peace between his red children and his white children. He was ready to make gifts to his red children and pay them money if they would sell part of their hunting grounds so they could be given to his white children.

The chiefs who were listening were there because they had been curious about what kind of a council a white man would call and what he would say. They sat quietly while St. Clair was talking. When he finished, most of them got up, shrugged their shoulders, and walked away. Their land had been given to them by the Great Spirit. They could no more exchange it for the white people's gifts and money than they could sell the air they breathed. The air was a gift from the Great Spirit, too.

But among them there were some young chiefs from the Wyandots, Delawares, Ottawas, and some of the small nations. They were greedy for the things the white man offered, and they had not yet learned wisdom. They put their signs on the governor's parchment and gave and received strings of wampum to seal the agreement to sell some of their tribal lands.

The young men went off and laughed among themselves. This foolish white man wanted to pay them for something he could never own. How clever they had been to profit from his foolishness! The time would come when they would hang their heads in shame for what they had done.

The governor sent the document off to Philadelphia to show the president. Washington looked at the names and knew that they were the signs of young men whose opinions were worth nothing.

As a young man, Washington had fought Indians, and he knew the respect that was given to warriors. Perhaps a show of military strength would succeed where the council had failed. A uniformed army with horses and cannons might impress the Indians so that they would agree to sell their land.

General Josiah Harmar was a soldier who had distinguished himself during the Revolution. At this time, he was a respected officer in the army and had been appointed commander-in-chief. Washington ordered him to muster an army and march into the Maumee Basin.

CHAPTER IV

A Taste of Victory

Little Turtle knew all about General Josiah Harmar's army almost as soon as it arrived at Fort Washington (the present site of the city of Cincinnati) on the Ohio River. Indian scouts watched and sent runners back to Little Turtle's camp with word that the army was made up of about three hundred regular soldiers and nearly five times that number in volunteer militiamen.

Most of the militiamen had been recruited in the east. They were untrained and unprepared for army life. Almost none of them had brought along his own kettle—a basic necessity for a soldier. They knew nothing about Indians or about forest fighting, and most of them were very young boys or old men. Nevertheless, they had no fear that it would be a simple matter to defeat any Indians they might meet.

Little Turtle smiled, and his dark eyes sparkled with mischief when he heard about the three shiny brass cannons the army had brought along. Cannons were fine for fighting on plains or for firing salutes in forts, but it would be quite a feat for General Harmar to get the heavy pieces across the rivers and through the forests where Little Turtle meant to lead him.

Fort Washington was built in 1790. It protected the little village that would grow up to be the city of Cincinnati.

The carelessness of the general surprised Little Turtle. After his arrival, Harmar and his officers settled down to enjoy the hospitality of Fort Washington instead of conditioning their men and training the raw recruits. The regular soldiers and the militiamen were left with nothing to do but drink up their rations of rum, quarrel among themselves, and waste bullets in shooting matches.

At that same time, Little Turtle was busy getting his warriors ready to meet the force of the federal army for the first time. He taught his men everything he had learned about the way the white men fought a war. He told them they must fight beside each other. Each man, regardless of clan or tribe, was to protect the left side of the man next to him. They must not try to count coup. The Americans

didn't understand it. When a warrior drew blood, he must
not withdraw from the battle. Instead, he must fight on as
long as he could. This enemy counted only *dead* warriors
and, if The People hoped to win back their stolen lands,
they must fight by the white man's rules.

The English were supplying the confederation with guns
and bullets, but Little Turtle did not reject the silent power
of bows and arrows. He used even the ponies as weapons
of war. Decorated with bells and streamers, they could
have quite an unsettling effect on the average army horse.

Little Turtle received the news that on September 30,
1790, General Josiah Harmar and his army had left Fort
Washington. They were marching north in search of Indians.

Harmar moved toward the Shawnee village of Chillicothe, which he destroyed. Then he heard of a large Miami
settlement at the place where the Maumee and the Auglaize
rivers met, and he set out in that direction. The cannons had
been left behind in the thick forests around Chillicothe.

Harmar arrived at the Miami village and sent a company
of militiamen under the command of Colonel Hardin to
capture it. They found that the Indians had already deserted
the place. Angry because there was nobody to fight with,
Hardin and his men burned all the houses and even set fire
to a storehouse that contained twenty thousand bushels of
corn.

The next morning, a soldier poking around in the ashes
of the village spied a faint trail leading away into the forest.
Harmar decided that that must be the way the Indians had
escaped. He ordered Colonel Hardin to take a company of
militiamen and go after them. The general was so sure of

himself that he neglected the first principle of forest warfare: always send out scouts ahead of your troops.

Little Turtle had selected the exact spot on which he meant to meet the Americans. He had a force of several hundred warriors hidden on the high ground that overlooked the river marshes. One half of his men were on foot and half were riding decorated ponies.

Colonel Hardin and the militiamen marched headlong into an ambush. Suddenly, they were surrounded by mounted Indians, covered with red and black war paint and yelling at the top of their lungs. The ponies, with the bells and the streamers, frightened the army horses so badly that they threw their riders and galloped off.

Then the Indians who were on foot closed in for hand-to-hand fighting. Most of the militiamen were killed. Colonel Hardin stayed alive only because he was lucky enough to fall into a swamp. He hid there, underwater, hoping the Indians would think he was dead. His enemies, however, knew just where he was, and they played a game with him. Every time the colonel came up for air, he saw one or more Indians standing around on the solid ground beyond the swamp. They kept him in the water until dark.

When Hardin, cold, wet, muddy, and frightened, finally made it back to Harmar's camp, he was horrified to learn that the general had heard the sound of the battle but had ordered the men he had with him to stay where they were. Kegs of rum went with every marching army, and that day the general had been drinking more than his share.

The next morning, the officers wanted to retreat and regroup but Harmar, still fuddled from his spree of the day before, refused. He chose to look on the Indian victory as

General Josiah Harmar, the first of three generals who would match their skill against that of Little Turtle.

a personal insult. Against the advice of his officers, the general sent out another search-and-destroy mission.

This time, some regular soldiers went along with the militiamen. Scouts brought word to Little Turtle as soon as the company left camp and, again, he set up an ambush. Indian sharpshooters had orders to pick off the officers and the regular army men. Major Wyily, one of the officers who commanded the regulars, fell with eighteen bullets in his body. The men who were left alive fled in panic.

The Americans had fought as bravely as they knew how, but they were badly led and most of them were untrained. They were no match for the highly organized and disciplined forces of Little Turtle. General Josiah Harmar, outfought, out-generaled, and facing mutiny among his few remaining troops, ordered a retreat to Fort Washington.

The Indian confederation had won its first major victory over the Americans. The united tribes were enjoying their triumph and their war chief was pleased, but he knew that there would be no time to relax. Pressure must be kept on the illegal settlers, driving them out of the Maumee Basin and discouraging new ones from coming in. And the Americans were sure to send in another army.

Little Turtle did not let his men grow confident and lazy. Constant practice kept their marksmanship sharp. At the same time, their families at home had to be taken care of. It is likely that in the lull after the battle, the men of the clans took turns going back to their villages to hunt so there would be meat to eat and furs for the women to barter.

Relays of scouts and runners ranged over the land from Lake Erie to the Ohio River. Anything that looked unusual or interesting was reported to Little Turtle.

In the late summer of 1791, word came to the camp of the war chief that another federal army was getting ready to march into Indian lands. This time it was General Arthur St. Clair, the governor of the Northwest Territory, who was in command.

St. Clair's orders were to march against the Indians, impress them with the military might of the United States, and urge them to sell some of their land. President Washington thought that Arthur St. Clair, an outstanding commander during the Revolution, might succeed where Harmar had failed.

General St. Clair was delighted with his assignment. More than anything, he wanted a chance to defeat Little Turtle in battle. St. Clair had never forgiven the war chief for not coming to his council.

With a force of twenty-four hundred men, the general marched into Indian country. He paused in his advance only long enough to build Fort Hamilton on the Great Miami River and Fort Jefferson at the joining of the Twin and Greenville creeks. He left stockpiles of weapons and supplies at both places.

The weather was good, and there was a picnic mood among the troops. Some of the officers, following the custom in European armies, had brought their wives along. In the baggage train of the army there were such unmilitary items as rocking chairs and china teapots.

St. Clair was careful to send scouts ahead, behind, and alongside his line of march. The trouble was that they could find no sign of the Indian army they were looking for. There would be an occasional glimpse of a warrior. He would let himself be seen just long enough to lead the Americans farther into the forest. Then he would vanish. The major force that St. Clair had hoped to meet seemed to have disappeared. He began to tell himself that it had been disbanded. Maybe the confederation had left the Maumee Basin altogether!

St. Clair couldn't have been more wrong. There were Indian scouts all around him. Runners were reporting every move the Americans made to Little Turtle. The war chief knew as much about General St. Clair as if he had seen inside his enemy's head.

Little Turtle knew that St. Clair was having trouble with his second-in-command, General Richard Butler. St. Clair was a proud man with an overbearing manner, and he was often rude to the younger man. Butler began to resent him.

Little Turtle was also aware of the bad feeling that had developed between the regular army men and the volunteer militiamen. They disliked each other so much that if a camp were set up beside a stream, they stayed on opposite sides. By late autumn St. Clair had been looking for the Indians for nearly three months. His men were bored and restless. The officers had become careless. They had even begun to take sides in the arguments between the general and Richard Butler.

Along with his other troubles, General St. Clair suffered constantly with rheumatism and gout. Cold weather made his ailments more painful, and he was eager to end the campaign. He sent half of his army back to Fort Hamilton with orders to set up winter quarters. He and the rest of the men would push on a little farther and see if they could find any Indians.

General Arthur St. Clair, governor of the Northwest Territory, who set out against the largest force of warriors Little Turtle could muster.

All these troop movements were reported to Little Turtle, and the war chief was satisfied. The general was acting just the way he had hoped he would.

On November 3, 1791, St. Clair's army made camp on the bank of the Wabash River not far from the present site of the town of St. Marys, Ohio. As usual, the regulars and the militiamen set themselves up separately.

It turned very cold, and the men did not take the trouble to build breastworks for the protection of the camp. All they wanted to do was roll themselves up in their blankets and go to sleep. Even General Butler neglected to scout the position before they settled in.

During the night, there was a light snowfall. In the early dawn, the soldiers began to move around to get warm. As they shook the snow off their blankets, their dark shapes made perfect targets against the whitened ground.

Little Turtle had been waiting all night for this moment. He ordered his men to charge. They swooped in from all sides with volleys of gunfire and showers of arrows. Whooping and yelling, the mounted warriors got between the Americans and their tethered horses and rode them down. Then the Indians who were on foot closed in for hand-to-hand combat.

General St. Clair did not even have time to put on his uniform. Wearing an old coat, with his white hair hanging in wisps under a tricorn hat, he tried to gather his troops to make a stand. The general was so crippled with rheumatism and gout that he had to be helped onto his horse.

Little Turtle had set up a command post on the top of a nearby hill. From there he could direct the action and get reports on how things were going. Every time General St.

Clair was able to rally his troops and drive the Indians back, Little Turtle had fresh bands of warriors ready to send in. He had the largest army the confederation had ever assembled at his command.

Panic spread among the Americans, who were only half awake. Indian sharpshooters picked off the officers and the regular army men. That left the green recruits with no one to lead them. The general himself had four horses shot from under him.

The battle in that wilderness began at six o'clock in the morning and lasted for three terrible hours. Finally, St. Clair, reduced to riding a pack animal, ordered a retreat to Fort Jefferson, forty miles away. The Indians chased the remains of the army for a short distance. Then they returned to the battlefield to pick up rifles, ammunition, and supplies and to round up the runaway horses that the army had left behind.

One of the warriors came back to camp carrying a feather tick, which was something like the fluffy down quilts we have today. He had never seen anything like it, but it was big and soft and it wasn't heavy. The other men began throwing it around, catching it, and falling on it. All at once, a seam in the ticking broke and the air was filled with feathers!

Feathers stuck to their bodies, got in their hair and eyes and even up their noses, making them sneeze. When they could stop laughing, the warriors said to each other that the Americans had brought along some strange supplies to fight a war. How had they planned to use all those feathers?

When General St. Clair retreated, he left behind more than a thousand dead and wounded men. All his officers,

General Butler among them, were killed. That three-hour battle with Little Turtle and the Indian confederation had cost the Americans more men and equipment than they had lost in any single battle of the Revolutionary War.

Little Turtle counted one hundred and fifty men killed and only a few wounded. The taste of victory was sweet, but Little Turtle did not rejoice. The People had won two battles, but they had not won the war. He had put his largest force in the field against St. Clair. If and when the Americans sent in another army, could he do it again?

At that time, Little Turtle, the great Miami war chief, was thirty-nine years old.

CHAPTER V

The Chief
Who Never Sleeps

For some time after the defeat of St. Clair, it looked as though Little Turtle and the Indian confederation were going to be successful in ridding their lands of the white invaders. Towns were emptying. Homesteaders were packing up and leaving. Boats bringing new settlers were no longer coming down the Ohio River.

Word of the victories of Little Turtle and the confederation had been carried to the nations in the Algonquin language family who lived in the east. Many young warriors from the Senecas, Mohawks, and other tribes of the Iroquois League made their way to the Maumee Basin. If the whites were to be defeated and driven out of the land, they wanted part of the glory. The presence of the young men led some of the chiefs to believe that the Iroquois League of Six Nations was ready to join the confederation.

The Miamis, Shawnees, Delawares, and other nations of the confederation began to believe that they would be free at last to go back to the sacred way of life of their ancestors. That belief was soon to be crushed.

In 1794, the United States government was being flooded with demands that American homesteaders in Indian lands have the protection of an army. Americans were eager for the rich lands of the Maumee Basin to be opened for settlement.

President Washington wanted to keep his promises to the Indians. If they would only agree to sell some of their land, all problems would be solved.

He appealed to the chiefs of the eastern tribes who belonged to the Algonquin language family. Washington promised to pay the eastern chiefs for their efforts if they would talk to Little Turtle and persuade him and the confederation to sell off some of their hunting grounds. The chiefs answered that the president would spend his money more wisely if he gave it to the would-be settlers for finding homes somewhere not in Indian territory.

Speeches began to be made on the floor of Congress, and the matter of Indian lands became political. Washington had no choice but to send in another army. This time he selected General Anthony Wayne as commander.

Once again, Little Turtle knew about the new army almost as soon as it was formed. He tried to find out everything he could about the new leader, and what he learned convinced him that this man was different from Harmar and St. Clair.

Anthony Wayne had been with Washington at Valley Forge. He was an experienced Indian fighter, who had defeated the Creek Indians in Georgia when they were allies of the British during the Revolution. Because of his love of danger, people called him Mad Anthony Wayne!

But Wayne was not "mad." He was a cool and careful commander. The more Little Turtle found out about the man, the more he realized that this new enemy was a lot like himself. Anthony Wayne planned every move in detail

General Anthony Wayne, whom Little Turtle called "the chief who never sleeps."

before he made it. So did Little Turtle. Wayne trained his men in forest fighting with the same methods that Little Turtle used. There were no china teapots or rocking chairs in Wayne's baggage train. The war chief and the American general had great respect for each other. If they ever met in battle, it was sure to be a contest between giants.

To test his enemy, Little Turtle set up ambushes. Wayne avoided every one of them. The Americans pushed their way into Indian country as far as the place where General St. Clair had been defeated. Wayne stopped long enough to bury the skeletons that were on the ground. Then he began to march again.

Little Turtle's scouts brought reports of the route the general was taking, but it didn't seem to be going anywhere in particular. The Indians began calling Anthony Wayne "The Black Snake" and "The Wild Wind" because they couldn't tell what he was likely to do next. Little Turtle realized that his own tactics were being used against him.

Finally, by a roundabout route, the Americans arrived at Fort Defiance, a stockade built at the place where the Maumee and Auglaize rivers come together and where General Harmar had been defeated. The town of Defiance, Ohio, is on the site today. Wayne settled in, and on August 1, 1794, he sent an offer of peace to Little Turtle and the confederation.

A copy of his offer went to the president in Philadelphia along with a letter in which he said he had reason to believe that this time the confederation would take the offer seriously. As he put it, "Everything they hold dear is at stake."

A young white man who had grown up with the Indians was Wayne's messenger. He came into the camp of the confederation and handed the peace offer to Little Turtle. He was to wait for an answer.

Little Turtle considered the offer very carefully. The army he had put in the field to defeat General St. Clair was the largest the confederation had ever been able to assemble. They could never do it again. At the same time, he knew that Wayne had a trained, organized army that was twice as big as the number of warriors the confederation could call up. Little Turtle was sure that, if the Indians should face this army in battle, they would meet certain defeat.

If the decision could have been made by Little Turtle alone, he would have accepted the offer and avoided bloodshed. All the chiefs in the confederation, however, had to vote on such an important question. A war chief was a leader, not a commander, and Little Turtle was war chief only by election.

He called for a council. Blue Jacket and Buckongehalos, his seconds-in-command, and William Wells, his adopted son, were beside him. Little Turtle told the chiefs,

"We have beaten the enemy twice under different commanders. Now the Americans are led by a chief who never sleeps!"

He reminded his listeners that their young men had tried to surprise Wayne many times and they had always failed. Day and night were the same to this American commander. Little Turtle said that something in his mind whispered that the Indians would be wise to listen to General Wayne's offer of peace.

Blue Jacket, the Shawnee who was noted for his short temper, flew into a rage. He shouted that Little Turtle was making the noises of a coward. The People were winning! Why did the war chief say they should accept peace now? Weren't the English still supplying The People with guns and bullets? Wasn't there a rumor that some of the eastern nations were getting ready to come to their aid? How many chiefs would agree with Little Turtle that the peace offer should be accepted? How many wanted to go on as they were—winning victories and driving the white invaders out of their country?

The speeches went on for another day but, in the end, the vote was loud for going on with the war. Wise men do not agree about whether Little Turtle was still war chief after the council.

Some voices say that he was put down and surrendered the council bag, the symbol of authority. Others say that he gave in and agreed to follow the will of the majority of the chiefs. In any case, his authority had been weakened. In the past, the confederation had acted as a unit, following plans laid out by Little Turtle. Now it broke apart with orders being given by any man who could shout louder than the others. That man was usually Blue Jacket, the Shawnee.

It was Blue Jacket who sent the confederation's reply to General Wayne. When Little Turtle heard about it, he knew that the chance for peace between the whites and the Indians had been lost. The Shawnee had sent a curt suggestion that the Americans remain where they were for the next ten days while the Indians decided on peace or war. Wayne was not the sort of commander to accept an answer like that!

Still another disappointment was in store for Little Turtle. William Wells, the young white man he loved like a son, had been talking to Wayne's messenger. Wells had played an important part in the battles against Harmar and St. Clair, but after meeting the messenger who, like himself, had been raised by the Indians, he began to feel guilty about fighting against white men.

Besides, he learned from the messenger that his brothers, whom he had not seen since he was eleven years old, were leading companies of militiamen from Kentucky and had joined Wayne. Wells knew he could not go into a battle in which his brothers would be on the other side.

Little Turtle had always known that the day would come when William would make the decision to return to his own people. He was not surprised when Wells asked to speak with him alone. They met at daybreak on the top of a cliff that overlooked the Maumee River. The two men faced each other in the grey light. The birds were just beginning to wake up when William Wells told his adopted father that the time had come when he must leave. He said,

"My father, let us be friends until the sun reaches its high place in the sky. From then on, we must be enemies. If you wish to kill me, you may. If I wish to kill you, I may."

The two men sat on the edge of the cliff, looking up and down the Maumee River. They talked until noon. Then they stood up, embraced, and walked away in opposite directions. Tears were running down their faces.

General Anthony Wayne received Blue Jacket's answer to his offer of peace on August 17. At once, just as Little Turtle thought he would, he ordered his troops to get ready to move out against the Indians.

Scouts brought word that the Americans were advancing rapidly along the Maumee, and Little Turtle made one last effort to bring the confederation back together. He knew that the Indians were outnumbered two to one. If they were to stand a chance of avoiding defeat, it had to be by the use of strategy. The enemy must be forced to fight in a situation where the Indians could put up the best defense.

He suggested that a small party of warriors should hold Wayne's army in check along the river and fall back slowly, drawing the Americans farther and farther away from their supply bases. In the meantime, a major force of Indians would circle around, ford the river at night, and come up on Wayne's rear and flank. The Americans would be caught in a box between the Indians and the river.

Only Tarke the Crane, a powerful Wyandot chief, saw the wisdom of Little Turtle's plan. Blue Jacket and all the others rejected it completely. Their past victories made them sure that they had no need for strategy. They could meet the Americans head-on and win!

So it was Anthony Wayne who selected the ground on which the battle was to be fought. On August 20, 1794, he chose to meet the Indians beside the rapids of the Maumee River on a stretch of land where a tornado had blown down most of the trees.

The Indians made hasty plans to use the fallen timbers as protection, but Wayne had a tactic of battle that they had never met before. As soon as his foot soldiers had used up the bullets in their guns, they didn't wait to reload. Instead, they charged the Indians with fixed bayonets.

The American cavalry followed the bayonet attack. With one hand holding the reins of their horses, they gripped sabers in the other and rode in, slashing right and left.

The Indians had no time to reload their rifles. They

The Battle of Fallen Timbers.

tried to use them as clubs, but they were no defense against the sabers and bayonets. The warriors pulled their own knives out of their belts, but they could not reach the bodies of enemies whose arms were lengthened by rifles with knives at the end. The sabers in the hands of the cavalry-men were heavier and more deadly than any weapon the warriors had ever used.

This battle had no rules and no courtesies. As Little Turtle had warned them, they faced an enemy who counted only *dead* Indians!

The Battle of Fallen Timbers lasted only forty minutes. When it was over, the Indians had no time to bury their dead. Wayne pursued the Indians who were left alive almost to the walls of Fort Miami, an English trading post fifteen miles from Lake Erie on the Maumee River. The Indians begged their allies for help, but the gates of the fort remained closed and locked. The English had no use for losers.

General Wayne headed back to his fort at Greenville on the banks of Greenville Creek in Ohio. He sent a report of the action to President Washington in Philadelphia which said,

"It is with infinite pleasure that I announce to you the brilliant success of the Federal army under my command!"

In another letter, he had described the lands of the Miami Indians. He said that every river bank looked like one long village. He added that he had never seen finer fields of corn and vegetables anywhere in the country.

On his slow march back to Greenville, General Anthony Wayne burned every village and destroyed every field he passed. No warning was given. Those Indians who escaped fled into the forest with only what they happened to have in their hands when the Americans came.

It was already September. Winter was only a matter of weeks away, and The People faced it with no shelter and no food. Even the stocks of furs they used for barter were gone.

CHAPTER VI

The Treaty
of Greenville

The Indians had never known such an evil time.
Every clan in the tribes was grieving over men who had
died in the Battle of Fallen Timbers, but there was no time
to carry out the formal ceremonies of sorrow. The People
had to make the most of every day of good weather that
was left to stay alive through the winter.

Their homes and storehouses had been burned; their
crops were destroyed. Their furs had been stolen or burned,
and since there was nothing left to barter, the traders
stopped coming. The cold weather was getting closer every
day, and The People had no walls to shelter them and no
food to put in their empty bellies.

They had grown to depend on the rifles the English gave
them not only for warfare, but also for hunting. When they
ran out of bullets for the few guns they had been able to
save from that last battle with the Americans, they begged
for more, but their former allies refused. Even in the coldest
part of the winter, when starving Indians dragged themselves to the gates of the trading posts and begged for food,
the English turned them away.

Little Turtle put his people to work making the weapons
their ancestors had used. He had them carve arrowheads

from the flint deposits in the Maumee Basin. They fashioned bows from saplings with deer sinews for strings. Finally, the Miamis had some weapons, but the large animals that they needed for meat had disappeared.

Foxes, wild cats, and panthers still roamed the forest, but their meat was not good to eat. Their skins could be made into clothing, but the animals themselves were hungry and much too dangerous to be hunted by a starving man armed with only a bow and arrows.

Sometimes, the hungry Indians were lucky enough to find some roots like wild potatoes or wild parsnips, and they could make themselves some bread. Otherwise, they were driven to robbing any squirrel's store of nuts that they could find.

Many men, women, and children did not live through that winter. Now that it was too late, the tribes realized how right Little Turtle had been when he advised them to accept General Wayne's offer of peace. Then they could have made a bargain with the Americans. Now they would have to make the best of whatever terms they were offered.

All during that terrible winter, Little Turtle tried to get a peace council set up. Time after time, he sent messages to General Wayne asking him to meet with the chiefs, but the General was busy building Fort Wayne in Indiana where it could command all the waterways flowing into Lake Erie. He always sent back the same answer—the general would not be ready to talk to the Indians until the middle of June. Then they must come to his headquarters at Greenville where he would call a council.

On June 16, 1795, the Indians began to gather outside the walls of the fort at Greenville. Many women and children came along because they were hungry, and the Americans had food which they would share. There were no old people and no very young children. They had all died during the winter.

By the middle of July, Little Turtle and the other chiefs of the broken confederation had arrived. One of the first people Little Turtle saw when he came to Greenville was his adopted son, William Wells. Wells was there as an aide to General Wayne and as an interpreter.

The two men met each other with the same old affection. Little Turtle understood the decision that had taken the younger man away from his side. Wells, in turn, was careful never to wear his American army uniform when he was with his adopted father. They were able to be comrades again.

General Wayne had built a council hut on "unbloodied ground" so the chiefs would have a place to speak with one another. As each chief arrived, he was given a string of white wampum as a sign of the general's good will. Peace talks began in earnest on July 20.

The Indians must agree to a new boundary line that would run diagonally from the place where the Cuyhoga River emptied into Lake Erie south across the Ohio River to the mouth of the Kentucky River, which the Indians call Cuttawa. All land south and east of that line, about twenty-five thousand square miles, must be ceded to the United States. The Indians would keep the area to the north and west. That meant that they would lose two-thirds of the territory Congress had given them in 1787—land that was to have belonged to the Indians forever!

At the same time, the United States would claim twelve

The monument marking the spot where the Treaty of Greenville was signed.

parcels of land, varying in size from two to twelve square miles in size, in the Indian reservation to be used for whatever purpose the government saw fit. The Indians would be allowed to hunt on the ceded lands as long as they offered no injury to a citizen of the United States.

The Indians were to be permitted to stop any white person from entering their territory, but they could not punish wrongdoers or settle disagreements on their own. Any dispute must be taken to the nearest Indian agent, who had been appointed to represent the government of the United States. The agent would be the one to decide who was right and who was wrong.

The Indians must promise to allow free passage between rivers in their territory, and they must swear that they would never sell any part of their reserved land to any government but that of the United States.

In return for agreeing to these terms, the Indians would receive supplies that would be worth $20,000 to help them recover from the past winter and get ready for the next. There was also the promise of an annuity, or yearly payment, of $9,500 to be paid to the nations and divided among the tribes. Prisoners of war would be exchanged.

Then Wayne surprised the chiefs by bringing out the treaty some of them had signed for General St. Clair at the Muskingum. He pointed out that portions of the land south and east of the new treaty line had already been sold to the United States. The U.S. government was claiming only what belonged to it!

The men who had put their signs on the document hung their heads. The gifts they had received from St. Clair were worn out or lost long ago, and the money had been spent. They had nothing left but their shame.

Little Turtle stood up. His dark eyes swept around the circle of chiefs and focused on Wayne. The expression on his face was pleasant and friendly, but he was determined not to give up one foot of Miami land without a struggle.

When he had everybody's attention, Little Turtle began to speak. He said the Miamis knew nothing about the treaty that Wayne had shown them. It had been signed by young men who had been dazzled by the promises of the white people. He said,

"You have pointed out to us the boundary you have set between the Indians and the United States. I take the liberty to say that the line cuts the Miamis off from a large part of the land where the print of our ancestors' houses are to be seen!"

Little Turtle reminded the chiefs and Anthony Wayne that the ancestors of the Miamis had lit the first fire at Detroit. They had extended their borders from the headwaters of the Scioto River to its mouth, down the Ohio to the mouth of the Wabash and over to the village of Chicago on Lake Michigan.

The Great Spirit had charged the members of the Miami nation not to sell or part with this land but to preserve it for their children. They were not to sell the land to any white man who wore a hat just because he asked for it.

"Elder brother," Little Turtle said to Wayne, "I have shown you the Miami country. Let me hear your answer. I will give you mine. I came hoping you would say good things. I have not heard them."

Wayne argued that the English and the French were also white men who wore hats. The Indians had already sold land to them. The Americans had captured that land from the English and French.

The chiefs went into the council hut where they all took turns speaking their minds. Some, like Tarke the Crane, the Wyandot chief, reasoned that since all land belonged to the Great Spirit, maybe the Americans had as much right to it as the Indians.

Little Turtle replied, "I had expected that we would all speak with one voice but there seem to be many thoughts. Take the time to quiet your minds. Consider what you are doing before you barter away the lands of our ancestors!"

The chiefs talked again with Anthony Wayne. The arguments the Indians offered were logical, well-thought-out, and clear. Wayne listened politely, but he refused to change a single phrase in his peace terms.

In the end, the memory of the past winter and the fear of the one to come caused the chiefs to accept what was offered. The People had to have food. Even their seed corn had been destroyed when Wayne burned their villages. Now the supplies would help them make a fresh start, and when they had the promised money, traders would come back and the Indians could buy what they needed.

On August 3, 1795, the Treaty of Greenville was ready to be signed by the Americans and the chiefs of the tribes in the Maumee Basin. A table was set up under a big tree outside the walls of the fort, and General Anthony Wayne, in full military dress, stood beside it. He was surrounded by his aides, interpreters, and scouts.

William Wells was there. The Indians trusted him to tell them the true meaning of any words in the treaty they did not understand.

The Indians formed a line. There were chiefs from the clans of the Miamis, Delawares, Wyandots, Shawnees, Potawatomis, and the smaller nations. Blue Jacket, the Shawnee, was there. So was Buckongehalos, the Delaware.

Little Turtle did not go to stand in the line with the others. He sat by himself off to the side.

General Wayne spoke to the chiefs. He said,

"Younger brothers, I take the war hatchet from your hands and, with a strong arm, throw it into the middle of the great sea where no man can ever find it. I give you the wide, straight path to be used by you and your children. As long as you follow this path, you will be a happy people!"

One by one, the chiefs came to the table. Some were still proud and defiant. Others were discouraged and heartbroken. As each chief handed over a belt of white wampum as a sacred symbol of his acceptance of the treaty and put his sign on the parchment, General Wayne presented him with a medal.

The medal was made of bronze washed with silver, about six inches long and four inches wide. One side showed President Washington, in uniform but bareheaded, handing a peace pipe to an Indian chief who was wearing the medal around his neck. They stood under a pine tree that had a tomahawk buried in its base. In the background, a farmer plowed a field. The inscription read, "George Washington, President, 1795."

The other side of the medal was embossed with the arms and crest of the United States on the breast of an eagle. In the bird's right talon was an olive branch to show the government's love of peace. Its left claw held a sheaf of arrows to indicate a readiness for war.

Slowly, the line of chiefs moved to the table under the tree. Three pieces of parchment, each twenty-six inches wide by twenty-five to thirty-one inches long, were there. Each man put his sign at the place he was shown by one of the general's aides and, with his medal and a copy of the treaty he had signed, went back to his place with his own tribe. Some looked as though they would have liked to throw the medal as far away as they could, but the memory of the past winter and the American promise of supplies and money to see them through the next made them have second thoughts.

As the line moved forward, Little Turtle stayed where he was, sitting as still as a statue molded in bronze. The look on his face was calm, even pleasant. His full, dark

*The medal that General Wayne gave each
of the chiefs who signed the treaty.*

eyes were fixed on a spot above the crowd. When the last
chief had left the table, Little Turtle still hadn't moved.

Silence settled over the crowd. It became so still that the
squirrels in the trees went back to chattering at each other.
Anthony Wayne began to get uneasy. He had a high regard
for Little Turtle, both as a fighter and a leader. If, at this
last minute, the war chief should refuse to sign the treaty,
everything might have to be done all over again!

Wayne moved restlessly. He was about to go over to the
place where Little Turtle was sitting, but William Wells
put his hand on the general's arm and signaled for him to
be patient. Wells remembered that his adopted father could
hide his strongest feelings behind a pleasant expression.
The shame of defeat that was being heaped on The People

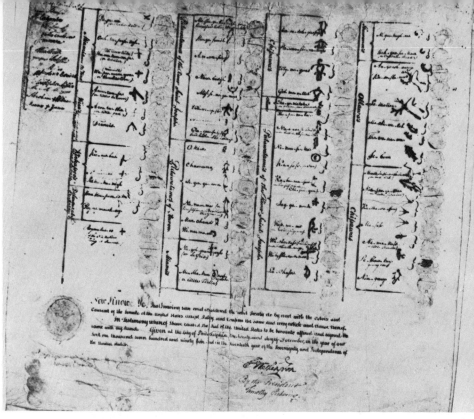

A photograph of the actual treaty.

must be tearing the heart of Little Turtle apart.

In his own time, Little Turtle stood up. He drew himself up to his full six feet of height and with great dignity walked to the table. He stood for a moment, looking down at the document of peace spread out before him. Then he added his sign to the others and handed over his belt of white wampum. In all, eighty-nine chiefs put their signs on the Treaty of Greenville. The Indian confederation was broken forever.

After Little Turtle has placed his wampum belt in the hands of Anthony Wayne, he stepped back, folded his arms, and looked directly into the eyes of the general. In a voice that was firm and clear, he said, "I am the last to sign this treaty. I promise I will be the last to break it!"

CHAPTER VII

A Country Gentleman

Little Turtle kept his promise. After he put his sign on the Treaty of Greenville, he never engaged in warfare against the United States again. Through his peace-keeping efforts, troubles between the Indians and the settlers almost came to an end. There were no more wars worthy of the name.

Little Turtle was given great respect among the Shawnees, Delawares, and the other nations as well as among his own people. He used his influence to encourage them to live at peace with their new white neighbors. Whenever a tribe grew restless and threatened to break the truce, Little Turtle was there, reminding them that the Indians had been defeated but not conquered! They would survive, but The People must not shed their blood in wars they could not win. Little Turtle even tried to advise the great Shawnee Tecumseh against his last disastrous effort to reclaim Indian lands.

Rufus King, an American historian, says that great honor is due the Indians. After signing the Treaty of Greenville, they never violated the limits it established. The same could not be said about the whites.

After the Treaty of Greenville was signed, the chiefs

waited around for the supplies that had been a part of the terms. It was already August, and they were eager to get home so they could prepare for the coming winter. The Indians began calling Anthony Wayne "General Tomorrow." Whenever they asked when they would get the promised supplies, his answer was always the same. "Tomorrow! Tomorrow!"

When the supplies finally arrived, they were too late and too few. The Indians were faced with another dreadful winter.

The People had thought that their new boundaries were secure, but to keep the peace and save the Indians further suffering, Little Turtle had to put his sign on three more treaties after Greenville. One was recorded at Fort Wayne in July 1803, the second was at the settlement of Vincennes in Indiana in August 1805. The third was at Fort Wayne, again, in September 1809.

Each treaty deprived the Indians of a little more land. They had become foreigners in their own country, subject to laws which they had no voice in making. For their own protection, they were forced to accept decisions made by invaders.

Little Turtle hoped the Indians and the whites might learn from each other. He urged his people to try some of the new things and methods the settlers were bringing in.

When he was a young man, Little Turtle had studied each new thing that the traders brought to his village. Now he showed the same interest in the farm animals and tools of the settlers. He studied the way they wove the wool from their sheep into cloth to make clothing, what they ate, and how they prepared and stored their food.

He was especially eager to understand the way they used the soil. The Indians had always used the *swidden,* a slash-and-burn method of farming. They would plant the same crop over and over until the ground was worn out. Then they would take down the houses in the village and move to another place where the earth was fertile. The white farmer used the same plot of ground to plant different crops in rotation so that the ground never wore out.

Little Turtle made a strong point of this difference when he advised the Miamis to change the way they managed their fields. It was important that there should be no more starvation winters like the ones before and after the Treaty of Greenville.

In the time of peace that followed Greenville, William Wells returned to the home of his adopted father and married Little Turtle's daughter, Sweet Breeze. Through the good work of Wells, the Miami chief received a large grant of the reserved land from the federal government and a guaranteed annual income. He shared both with the Miami people.

Wells helped Little Turtle build a permanent home on the bank of the Maumee River, about twenty miles from Fort Wayne. It was a real cabin instead of a longhouse. Alongside it there was a barn for horses, a cow, a few pigs, and some chickens that the settlers were teaching Little Turtle to take care of. The fields around the buildings were planted, cultivated, and harvested according to the ways he was learning from the whites.

In his turn, Little Turtle taught the settlers how to dry and store corn the Indian way and how to get a double yield from a field by planting corn and beans in the same bed. He explained which of the forest animals were good for food and which were useful only for their skins. He showed them how to tap a maple tree for the sap that could be boiled down to make sugar.

Little Turtle did all this to show The People by example that they could have a good life by trying new things and new ways. In the beginning, his barn was burned a few times by roving bands of rebel Indians. To them, a barn—anybody's barn—was meant to be burned.

Each time he built a new barn, more Indians came to see how it was done. Some went home and tried to do it themselves, and others accepted Little Turtle's invitation to live on his grant of land. A village grew up around the farm belonging to the former war chief.

Little Turtle was a friendly man who liked to be with all kinds of people. He enjoyed the bustle of the city of Philadelphia, and he went there many times. Sometimes he went alone, and sometimes William Wells went with him. By that time, Wells was a captain in the United States army.

When Little Turtle was in the city, he put aside his deerskin clothing and his blankets and dressed like all the other men. The tight pantaloons stuffed into calf-high boots of soft leather, the cutaway coats with high collars, the fancy waistcoats, lacey jabots, and low-crowned hats with narrow rolled brims that were fashionable looked well on his tall, slender figure. When he walked down a Philadelphia street or went to a party, admiring looks followed him.

Little Turtle became very popular in what then was the nation's capital city. When he was in town, he received more invitations than he could possibly accept. The war chief had learned to dance as gracefully as any Philadelphia gentleman.

Little Turtle had so many friends in Philadelphia that he was urged, over and over again, to make his home there. But he always went back to his farm on the Maumee River. He told those who insisted that although he enjoyed his visits, all his city friends lived inside the walls of their shops and offices. His greatest hope was to take their minds outside the walls and show them the world as the Indians saw it. As long as he lived, Little Turtle worked for mutual respect and understanding between the Americans and The People.

He died quietly at his home on the Maumee River on July 14, 1812, and never knew that all his efforts to protect his people were eventually to fail. In 1846, the Miami nation was forced by the U.S. government to move from the Maumee Basin to the dusty plains of the western United States. They followed the Cherokees along what became known as "The Trail of Tears."

In the long view of history, Little Turtle counted coup against his greatest enemy, General Wayne, after all. In the early part of the twentieth century, the mayor of the city of Fort Wayne, Indiana, was J. M. Wolcott. Mr. Wolcott was the grandson of William Wells and the great-grandson of Little Turtle!

Nobody knows the exact place where Little Turtle is buried, but there is a monument to his memory on the site of his home on the Maumee River, about twenty miles northeast of Fort Wayne.

The original parchments of the Treaty of Greenville with the signs of Little Turtle and the other eighty-eight chiefs of the confederation are preserved in the National

The Signing of the Treaty of Greenville *by Howard Chandler Christy.*

Archives in Washington, D.C. The Smithsonian Institute, in the same city, has a portrait of Little Turtle. It is a steel engraving and shows him as he looked about the time he signed the Treaty of Greenville.

At the top of a stairway leading from the rotunda of the state capitol building in Columbus, Ohio, there is a giant canvas painted by Howard Chandler Christy. It is titled *The Signing of the Treaty of Greenville,* and everybody is in the picture—Blue Jacket, Buckongehalos, Anthony Wayne, and William Wells. The dominant figure is that of Little Turtle. He is shown in the act of holding up a belt of wampum and making his vow, "I am the last to sign this Treaty. I promise I will be the last to break it!"

THE AUTHOR

A free-lance writer and commercial artist, Maggi Cunningham has written many short stories, including stories about native Americans, for children's magazines. She has also written *The Cherokee Tale-Teller,* published by Dillon Press.

She spent her childhood in Washington State, North Dakota, and Minnesota—states with a rich Indian tradition—to which she credits her interest in native American culture. Ms. Cunningham was educated at Saint Margaret's Academy in Minneapolis, Saint Mary of the Springs in Columbus, Ohio, and Ohio State University. She is now living in Columbus.

The photographs are reproduced through the courtesy of the Field Museum of Natural History, Chicago; the Garst Museum, Greenville, Ohio; the Indiana Historical Society Library, Indianapolis; the Minneapolis Public Library Athenaeum; and the Ohio Historical Society, Columbus.

OTHER BIOGRAPHIES
IN THIS SERIES ARE

William Beltz
Robert Bennett
Black Hawk
Joseph Brant
Crazy Horse
Geronimo
Oscar Howe
Pauline Johnson
Chief Joseph
Maria Martinez
George Morrison
Daisy Hooee Nampeyo
Michael Naranjo
Osceola
Powhatan
Red Cloud
Will Rogers
Sacagawea
Sealth
Sequoyah
Sitting Bull
Maria Tallchief
Tecumseh
Jim Thorpe
Tomo-chi-chi
Pablita Velarde
William Warren
Annie Wauneka